J.J. Moon is a Riyadh born, poet who lives somewhere beneath a dune. She is an avid traveler, horse rider, paint splatterer, and storyteller. She does most of her poetry writing late at night, inspired by events of the day and the people she has met on her journeys, both short and long. She writes to understand people and herself; she is still confused.

Coughing Up Ash

J. J. MOON

AUSTIN MACAULEY PUBLISHERS

LONDON • CAMBRIDGE • NEW YORK • SHARJAH

Copyright © J. J. Moon 2021

The age group that matches the content of the books has been classified according to the age classification system issued by the National Media Council.

ISBN – 9789948834755 – (Paperback)

ISBN – 9789948834762 – (E-Book)

Application Number: MC-10-01-6678744

Age Classification: 21+

Printer Name: iPrint Global Ltd

Printer Address: Witchford, England

First Published 2021

AUSTIN MACAULEY PUBLISHERS FZE

Sharjah Publishing City

P.O. Box [519201]

Sharjah, UAE

www.austinmacauley.ae

+971 655 95 202

"To the many selves I have been and to my soul friend,
thank you."

Coughing Up Ash

My blood flows like sandpaper on bones,
no amount of scratching will rid the itch
of you.

I tried to cut
you out of me.
Morphing into my breath,
you fill the space in my lungs, choking me.

Ad hoc, I tied knots-ties, tried
sniffling from poppy seeds,
tearing out the stem from leaves,
nothing will rip you out.

Then stillness falls upon me,
an engulfing macrophage of sobriety.
I reside, soot-covered
and still.

While my old form falls
off, in ash.
Scales are burns, of pealed skin
I am Sybil, sin.

Kuklos, by infringement
of demons eating their human flesh,
plucking their feathers
Hecate, I am born.

Where demons lurk, crawling on crackling floors
in the house of souls.
With too long a wish-list to stop by my door
twice.

Slinking underneath another's door.
Inside, personified feelings morph.
Wall by wall,
one after the other, little Liliths are born.

Dear Baba

(وَإِذَا الْمَوْءُودَةُ سُئِلَتْ * بِأيِّ ذَنْبٍ قُتِلَتْ)

سورة التكوير

The name you gave me
is what people call my moving bones.
I often think of when my sins will be reckoned
by what name will I be called forth?
On the day when all I am is laid bare—
will demons pull me to hell from my hair?
For the misfortune of being born a female
one-fourth of an heir.

Baba, these words I have written you
are ones all my sisters share
hidden like my face behind a scarf,
even though it's men who stare.
I hid and bid my time to preserve my image
in your mind.
Baba, you taught me to feel scared.

To curl up like a feline
that's been locked in a room
for too long,
because you think I belong to you—

my honor lies on a bed,
Baba, I feel dead.
Cover, cover, cover your head,
they told me to whisper because men
get aroused, it's my fault I exist
so, my words aren't heard
but will you allow for them to be read?

Baba, you've covered me
I don't exist,
maybe that's the point
my fingertips on your beard, Baba,
I thought you loved me?
I'll see you on judgment day.
Good bye, till then.

Grafted Politics

Heathen, heathen, I'm heaving
Mutawaas are chasing me down streets
putting up partitions,
taking down posters
in the image of anything living.
Faith has been priced,
too high to be afforded.
Only a few are born worthy of heaven,
hell is not a place you need to wait to die to be in
just look within, parts of you are searing.
These grafted politics destroy us
when the men in charge make decisions
sawing off our fingers and replacing them with toes.
Necrosis,
interpreting God's words according to their politics
pockets of money, where did it come from?
and yet I am the heretic.

Anarchist,
nothing we try to put in our hands are we able hold.
Debridement,
crippling our human bodies.
The men in charge have left us disfigured
claiming we were born malformed,
they continue to saw off parts of us.

Panda Effect

He needs your applause to feel seen
the panda man can have whatever
the panda man needs.
He is all powerful,
a predator unmatched.
He has grown fat.
To him, I am a little rat
disposable, meat,
to be experimented on
and trapped.
He, on the other hand
has grown accustomed to luxury.
He only eats bamboo,
just the tip of the shoot.
The rest is beneath him
and his fine-boned jaws.
Served on a golden spoon
he has forgotten the use of his claws.
You can hear me scurry on my paws
for fear of being eaten,
he has forgotten the purpose of trying,
he has stopped mating.
The panda man is entitled,
unaware, of a world without him,
he is on the verge of extinction.

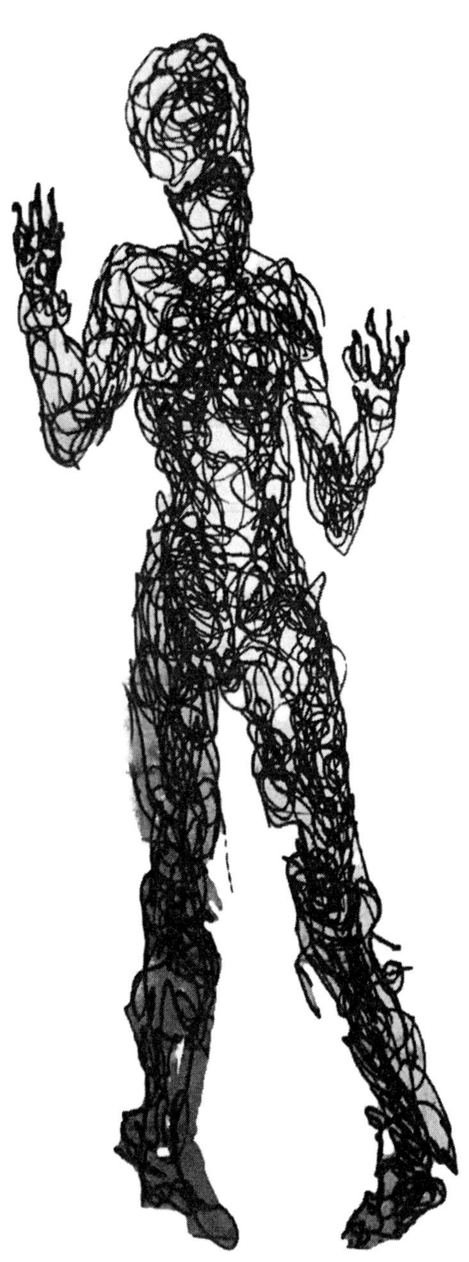

Sand Castles

We build our empire on sand and stone
while the winds rave over,
chipping and seizing
satchels of gravel as their currency.

Time has a taxation,
while the sand man comes,
to lull us.

Taking tax, filling up his bag,
هبوب comes calling,
she is unseen wrath.

نسمة

glides by, her steps can't be heard
she whispers laughing
we forget ourselves in her.

هبوب returns for us in our sleep,
she slips past our sheets
with no knifes, swords, or spears,
we are ripped out of our homes.

while Petra stands,
telling the tale of plucked-out palm trees
the River Jordan will not protect us.

our sands drift off our shores
the empire falls into grain
carried by the currents into another sea
bed for others to wake and build,
what was once ours.

Chartered Company

I heard you fear
men with bombs blowing up
your doors, fear not
the forsaken.
People die of greed,
too. It eats up your innards
till it reaches skin.

The land will fill and reclaim
bodies crushed beneath
the earth's pressure,
black gold
the nomads drift past dunes
as clouds, a man explores fortune
with an intellect for bending truths.

Glutinous, he digs, teaching the less-adapted about the
oil rig
he reaches a well,
scraping up a cup
of thick muck
he gulps it down.

Zomë, east of *Zamzam*.

A savior
to the Bedouin band
he splurges his wealth,
the band digs through dunes
as he stands,
and chucks up another cup.

Reclaiming his land,
while the chiefdoms fight
with bombs and swords,
heads on pikes.
He chucks up cups.

The explorer is dead.
A kuru cup, he lays
Jaw-gapping, black-toothed,
and blue-skinned.
Buried beneath the desert dunes
under the pressure of rocks.

On the surface, nomads drift.

Diamonds Galore

He gave me a ring, twinkle
I love it. I love him,
everyone says it's drop dead.

Except for it being blood-rimed
at the crack,
where the diamond's soldered to the ring.

It came, it comes however it may
I, redheaded, will rise diamond-dressed
through forks in my hair galore.

I pitch it forth in hay,
nay, heaven's fields need not
a pitcher to throw the straw.

The lord is my shepherd
glitter is his light
upon a mountain or in cave.

I, we, send forth grumpy and dopey
best friends, to the birds, with axes
carbon to light carbon to take.

In the end, diamonds
are a girl's man's girl's
only friend.

Branding Religion

The lord is my shepherd and I am his sheep
or so I have heard.
The preacher has branded religion
on my skin
and on the others' too.
BA-aaa BA-aaaa BA-aaaa.
It hurt at first, but he fed us.
Despite the burn of the rode
and the crispy hair in the place
where there should have been a tuft.
BA-aaa BA-aaa BA-aaa.
A hungry mouth can forget the truth.
We were told 'grass isn't always greener
on the other side,'
while being bred for our meat.
The wealth of a nation or a corporation
is all in the brand.
BA-aaa BA-aaa BA-aaa.
Religion has been marketed
by the preacher,
and faith put to good use.
We sheep, are consumers
to be consumed.
Ba.

Palm

For the king I pledged to love and the queen I aimed to be
I fed my blood to the sycamore tree
my heart was the beating seed of the land
I ripped out my voice and they chopped off my hands.
My words stitched to the winds
screeched love for my country man
while fate lay in the palm of fighting clans.
When autumn came, the trees' veins
spurt out my blood to every leaf
reminding all, summer came with a price
but winter brought oblivion, and the devil's vice.
Hungry, gluttonous, they fed off the fruit I bore
spring was the temptress; the sacrifice was ignored.
Valhalla, they seemed to preach getting off on summer's
heat but in the way, stood the carcasses of undying love.
Over it, the clans stepped and kept spewing blood.

Oh, Little One

Goodnight, sleep tight under a blanket of snow
your eyes will shut as cows jump
over the moon, spoons behind your back.

Oh my days, oh my days
I lost the knife
in the cow's back, now the moon is bloody.

Rest, rest,
I'll kiss your eyelids, shut
but Wendy darling is aching to jump.

Not now, says the dish to death,
cracked, miss spoon is missing
the dog's still laughing.

The cradle comes down
with a thump, and crack
Wendy leaps out the window.

Child

Under a blanket of snow
we make an igloo home
I made you a potato—
patch doll.

Maybe next week, a cabbage
one, will pop out of the ground
but now,
your milk teeth are falling off.

The tooth fairy can't travel this far.
Dear darling, I have told you so many times
to stay inside, don't step or touch cracks
or look up at the sky.

It's bad luck, like walking outside
going into town, turning your palm up.
I know you wanted a blanket so we can play ghosts
but you aren't allowed to play that game.

Darling,
I got you three matches.
No, we can't stop playing pretend.
Sell the first two and we'll use the third.
Why did you light them all?
You're smiling at me,
but I wish you would stop,
this isn't part of pretend.

Covered under a blanket of snow.

Dear Mama

I am on a train far away.
I pass the walls and gates of your haven.
Turpentine spilled on a rococo painting.
Soon

You'll hear them call out the news.
Rigged, I am the tar-tainted sinner
with the first breath of thought
I started to lie.

Laying all sheaths of culture aside
I stitched a cloak on my own
and wondered, through
asphalt-paved streets
a naked path.

The outskirts, unknown was a mirage.
I needed to quench, something
my fingers would linger on
but never touch.
I have learnt to carry the burn.

Dear Mama,
I apologize for not stitching the quilt.
I hopped on a train
leading to the sky or sea.
Fire begot light.
Dear Mama, you will always be dear to me.

You left

You left me
With your ashes in an urn
You left me,
Without the memory of words that
needed to be said
you left me,
with images hacking the sanity
of what's left of my nerves
you left me,
with my fingers tugging at the roots on
my head,
nap red from nail marks
you left me with the smell of carbon
following me wherever I go
you left me,
with that last look in your eyes
you left me,
with an empty
pill box, tissues box
no box of hope
to open
you left me with the image of you
and tubes shoved down your throat, you left me
wondering, why I wasn't enough
you left me and I didn't want you gone
you left me
wishing I could have left you first.

Stand

The masochist has married the sadist
in the company of a suitable pair
what a mixture of pleasurable power and despair
he takes out his stick and she offers her wrists
smiling, loving, adoring with all that she bares.

Bow your head but stand up straight,
didn't anyone teach you?
it's not lady-like to have a voice or make a choice
have your own name or make a claim.

So revel in her blood, and rejoice.
You ogre, feast, you beast.
It is your right to marry the mad.
The female is stereotyped alectis up to this time.

Forgiving, and giving her soul for that of a pig.
At the apex, look back and think, you martyr,
was he worth the trouble and shame?
Live strong, live on.

The Upper Hand

He came back home today
washed his hands
picked up a plum
sunk his teeth,
the juice dripped
and trailed, down
his webbed chin.
He walked by my mother
who was chopping.
He was staring at her
hands, pouting,
spewing:
'Your fingers' nails
unfeminine.'
She retorted,
'Darling, darling, darling,
I'll fix them.'
Through grunts and grumbles
his semi-human sounds
he turns to me
about a
'Job, move out
too many mouths.'
He plumps down
starting at his cuticles

Bear

This form I have was built to bear,
to break bone, expanding
flesh-tearing, bringing life into a world
that rejects all things female.
I am starting to pull out my hair
rather than cover up
or
strip down.
It's all the same. When a man's urges
dictates my appearance
based on his cultural preference.
People ask me why I am so angry
it's because I never got a puppy
and grew up to realize that I
was meant to be one
to a man.
Where he tells me what to do
and I listen and obey.
Nay, I won't do it.
According to you
I am stubborn and difficult too.
Forgive me, but I pray to no man.

Regardless of what you preach
I don't need your vindication.
You don't get to declare
my eternal damnation
because I won't cover my hair
or give you an heir.
I feel the blood within me laying
heavy like a burden.
It has stopped flowing, clotting
at the heart.

Bouquets

You disappoint me
in so many ways,
I am done pretending,
you'll have an umbrella to give
on a rainy day.
You disappoint me.
So, I gave you bouquets
I hope you'll see it's worth it
for you to stay.
But you'll disappoint me
till the very last day.

Now I give myself bouquets.

Galatea

Draw and quarter your own skin.
Tis treason to be different,
to feel odd things
when they say look down
but you look up, expect—
the executioner's cut.

It may not be a blade
but the fragile ties
of human,
of human,
love.
It will hurt just as much.

It will hurt, like they tied you to stone
and watch you drown.
Let the chisel cut the parts of you
you thought you needed, to function.
We are all Pygmalion—
unable to love what we cannot alter.

A Bag of Flesh

I am lost inside my skin
within, a bag of flesh;
a container to my soul.
It weighs heavy like a clump.
I move,
Thump, thump.
I feel the weight of my blood
Somewhere, in this clump
of a form, that is associated with a name,
given to me, or so states
the paper and pen
in a file, a record, that I exist.
Despite,
what lays beneath all that is,
is nothingness
and yet we strive to own,
objects, and things,
like this stuff of owning our skin,
titles and words to attach
to our paper-given names
reputation, legacies, honor
are just words, words, words,

and I bare it, like a burden,
that was stitched to my skin
while this bird within me shrieks
from being held in my ribs
it's inner egg simmers
in life's murky waters.
The soft-boiled egg inside me
turns to rot.

Beneath It

She had a fascination with scars,
droplets of blood,
smears on sweaters,
and carpet stains,
but mainly peeling skin,
chaffing off layer by layer,
like reaching a fruit's juicy center,
out it dropped, tinkering,
and spilled.
There was so much more substance,
inside no one could see,
she,
would show them, by cutting and peeling,
layer and layer,
pouring out, till all that was inside her, reached air;
everyone would breathe her in.

Shadows

There are shadows in mind
dark silent moving things
they don't speak
but lurk,
in corners,
shading my corneas.

There are shadows in mind
that create images when I think
they dance behind my thoughts
and cling to my feelings.

There are shadows in mind
they are always there
they linger as I blink
only in moments when the sun is bright
do they shrink.

There are shadows in mind
they crawl over my thoughts
shrouding them in darkness
growing, till, I can't see

everything turns into nothingness.

All That Lives Must Die

He came at night whispering words with the winds
through teeth blackberry stained,
cloths touched by rains
he told me to wait.

He climbed up the crawlers and brought news
the moon refused to tell.
She only reflected what she chose,
the rest shadows ate.

She deemed him beneath me,
everyone was to her,
her locks of white glowing hair covered my skin, nour-
ishing me.

He remained in the shadows whispering
each night he came, his voice once a whir;
became louder and more distinct.
She told me to be but he asked me to tell.

At the needle stuck in my arm, he sometimes would
stare
I'd catch his glances,
mirrored on his glistening scythe.
She'd tell me not to succumb.
Soon all she was,
was a whisper; a whir of incompressible words.
as her light would fade, his voice would grow
she kept shedding hair.
So I lay in my bed
as he cuts away each strand of hair,
silently I wilt and wait,
for him to reap me.

Holly

The holiness of a body
that keeps breaking
in service of another
for the sake of his pleasure
at the price of her honor
she,
embraces the ascetic of damage,
he traces his finger on the carnage of
what was once human skin—
that could feel.
He leaves the room, she is emptied out
into something worthless
the feeling is contagious
like contracting syphilis,
be careful who you kiss.
He stole her reflection from mirrors
for months she stared at a blank mirror
despite following the book's instruction
of binding her toes back
rib bones in,

she should feel perfect
but the image she looks at
is mocking her.
She has nothing to offer
but a powdered face.
He is gone, stole—
her belief in grace
she doubts—
her existence in a world
where he walks out—
in the light
going back to a home
while she is bound—
to the night.

Spring Has Ended

Like a little scab I'd like to
peel off.
your soul swarms up
onto the earth
Hades capturing Persephone
you will be the death of me.
This hurt sits like a clump of tissue
in my chest
hatred is slimy and sticks to everything.
Your eyes are staring at me
gray as a rainy London day
moist, in an uncomfortable way
covered in rot, ash, soot
falling unto everything I own
I live with demons that sleep
in my head.
They are waiting in my bed
unclenching your fists
you come to me with fingers crawling
like you own my meat
I paint these feelings
with the grime of my soul
A rope of skin or clump of hair
he has pulled out a tuft.
By all that is visceral

cochineal red
of feelings that are too heavy to carry
they spill out of me like a blood splatter
of words on paper
I carry the burden
within my blood from limb to limb.
My foot drags
and words slop over my tongue
my eyes glaze over endless pages
the feeling remains too heavy
for this body to carry.

Misery

Misery, I know your name
you have been in my bed
traced your fingers across my face.

Misery, I know how you taste
like salt forced down my throat
you are what it feels like to be unsafe.

Misery, you deceived me
I felt you inside me
whether on top or beneath.

Misery, you feel like nothingness
you feel like emptiness
no matter what you do or say.

Twinkle

Twinkle, twinkle little star
I think you have taken this game a
little too far.
The only rule I was given
was that I can't say no.
This lie I carry with me
wherever I go.
Riddle me diddle,
he fiddled with me.
I have wished upon a thousand stars
to rid me of these love bite scars.
He's lurking in the background
waiting,
for a chance to come in.

Latent

He is in the room,
it's always assumed he isn't.
He is right there
by my side, breathing down
my neck.
He touches my back
each vertebra crackles
my clavicles expand
shoulder blades touching
but he stays, behind me, attempting
to massage the soreness.
Juniper, he says:
'Bring red tea,' gripping me,
'bread would do on the side.'
An Adam, one of many
sits, flipping
pages.
Skimming through
skipping, lines,
words,
to be understood in context.
He is digging, into my tissue,
his fingers so round feel sharper
slicing through
taking his tea

and watching me
he moves to the end of the room
slurping.
The knife glides through the bread
I can still feel the imprint of his grip
crunching.
He is grunting and mumbling
'Have you read?'
Still standing there
'What happened, Juniper?'
I wonder why, he is standing
'I tripped.'
Behind the door crack peeping through
'Be careful'
he smiles, quietly
why are some smiles heard?
Others hushed, I walk back and
open the crack in the door.

Bite

You can keep biting me, darling
taking out chucks of my meat
ripping into my flesh
carving, my human form to eat.

You can keep biting me, darling
have my blood spill and taint
your cheeks
cutting out parts of me piece by piece.

You can keep biting me, darling
have my veins stuck between your teeth
let my blood gush down your throat
feel the warmth of my heat.

You can keep biting me, darling
even if I scream
with half my face gobbled up
and only bone is left to see.

I know that taking it all from me
makes you feel strong,
so, you can keep biting me, darling
through all the pain, I am human
and you a monster that needs to feast.

Freudian Slip

Through the breadth of human capacity for language
and words,
all he has ever learnt
is to say 'fuck.'
He uses is profusely as his only adjective,
imposes it on all his nouns and turns it into a verb.
Impishly, he swings from the vines of sentences,
expressing himself with 'fuck'—
'fucked,' 'fucking,' 'fucker,' 'fuckerrucking.'
No doubt, a continual Freudian slip.
Though grant it the word holds its weight.
Sometimes I feel like throwing a dictionary at you
with hopes the words will pour into your mind.
Or perhaps I enjoy the idea of tomb hitting you.

A Serpent Dream

Everything you have done sits
on me like spit.
I still remember,
the shape of your fingertips moving
over and inside, my body
but not how they felt on my skin—
thin, from chaffing and soiled
something fresh has gone spoilt,
throttled and wrung to be consumed.
Then the memory comes
like a snake crawling over my body,
at night in dreams, I see you.
I awake to the sound of hissing and slimy skin
I know,
you'd been here, it was real;
you left behind,
your molten human skin,
you hissed a kiss.
The toilet seat comes down.

Voice

He's coming tonight, perhaps by moonlight
his shadow casts shades on chandeliers
my childish fears are swept away with the sea's flow
I've lost my voice, I have no choice, I'll follow you
weed black hair, my feet merge, you pull me under
I drown in dark blue, it scathes and scars
I unpeel my skin, I'm drowning in sin
the air spits at me, I am banned from my land
your voice was so sweet but
now the water fills my lungs
suffocating, I morph into scales
my blood is slime, I slip, I slither
A tomb of water.

Ouroboros

Scathing, descaling your skin
you stand impotent,
in your own disgrace
nay, not by measure
of your inability to lift what lays
between your legs
but,
by your heart's ineptness
within me, lays warm blood that rushes
through to my lips
longing for warm kisses
but I dread,
the hiss of your tongue
when it touches mine
cold-blooded; you think that makes you strong
reptilian in your ways
underdeveloped mind, can't fathom that
of an empathizing mammal kind,
one that longs for more than to, just, mate
like a bundle of snakes
to slither and belly crawl up to your prey,
rattle song jaw-gaping—
open wide
snap shut
fangs pressed down,

venom spreads into a warm-blooded heart
you live to consume and procreate
till, one day you see your own tail,
without realizing you are a snake,
unfamiliar, it becomes your next prey.
Open up and push out those fangs
straighten your gaze
and let the shimmer of your own skin
woo you in, closer,
and closer, you, draw up to your self
open you go, unable to feel the bites
you take upon your own end.
In a ring, a cycle of your ruthlessness
is a fate you weaved,
go ahead, don't love, don't feel.

Bitter Taste

Bitterness is a taste that is acquired
like a tongue sloping over a lemon
acridity, coats all feeling
then, starts the craving
for what is lacked,
in forms that can't sustain
the human system
a need for love stemming
from scarcity
drives his gluttony.
He has learnt to season his food
differently
the meat is dried
vegetables pickled
like a heart that needs to be preserved
and stored away.
He offers his love in rations,
but it expires without use
unknowing, the taste of what is warm
and sweet without aching or raging
hunger set to destroy and ravish
what it can get its hands on
he presses into women
from the desperation of a loveless life
craving the taste of what is lacked.

Dew

The leaves have changed colors.
The wind has a new tune.
I look for sustenance in my cupboard.
But you ate all the food.

I know you'll stay past autumn
when nights tread on a little long for you.
But I am the female lead in the princess and the pea.

You are now the pea.

Curdled

Your proclaimed love disappears like dew
in the morning
and I shiver in a soft blue sweater,
with wide holes
unsuitable for this weather.
My love pours out like curdled milk,
the bread we share between us
is now stale
while
the residue of thought and feeling remain
like a coffee stain, cookie crumbs
crumpled napkins,
on a dish that was once served
while questions arise,
why?
Silence, at the edge of the begging and bartering
with diamonds and salt
when the world has moved to a new currency,
it's over.
Yet, we retained the aftertaste.

Fiscal Bonds

Dear un-estrangable husband
you may tell me what to do
have the last say in what I wear
and what I do with my hair.
You may control every aspect of my day
demanding that I cook for you, work for you
while you are the hand the force feeds me
and holds mine at the wrist.
I swear If I could leave, I would
but as you know, and made sure to see
my finances are tight
I don't fancy living rough
or watching you squander
the little one's assets on your version of a 'fun' night
but dear, your appetite is insatiable
not just when it comes to girls your daughter's age
you are quite likely to die of gluttony
and I will continue to deep fry your food
just the way you like it,
after all, you have the last say
and dearest husband,
on that frightfully joyous
much-awaited day

I swear,

I will dance all over your grave.

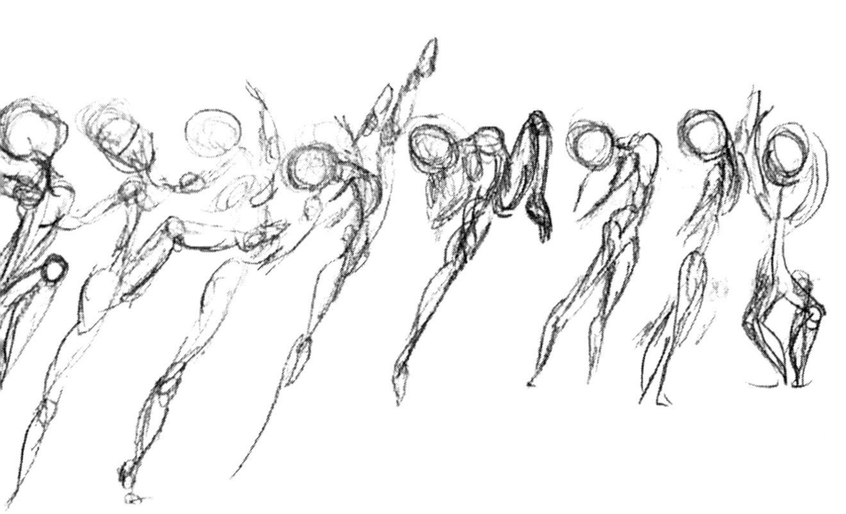

The Patriarch

Running away from the patriarch
I hoped we could become estranged
you see, he hooked my foot to the ground
a captain he declared himself
while everyone else was a lost boy.
He turned into a green-eyed crocodile
because he couldn't fly
but my heart leapt out
with the blowing wind
and swept past
hanging linen
to a dream his mind
would never know.

I have seen you   in her arms,
Enough
I have heard you   saying her name,
Enough
I have felt you   **Enough**   pulling, pushing
Enough
I have tasted you   without understanding
Enough
I can still smell you   haunting me
Enough
I have learnt.

I relapse back into that s-S-S-sh-i-f\f\-t-T-t
and the flash backs start
creating rifts within my mind I start sc^ccccrat^ttching.
Then the memories barge in
unannounced.
I remember, you thinking,
I couldn't tell—
you'd been s-sn-i-f\f\-***-ing around
your fingers on my thighs
and other
places, they shouldn't be
mocking me,
you, lifting up

your shirt at the sight of every mirror
trigger,
should I have given you a moment
alone?

Ash, falling, ass;
there was no s p ace in you

for a heart

–because of your six pack–
in you for a mind

nothing to show beneath it.

Then I hear your voice.
Remmmmmmmembering,
crossing streets with your hand
clenching mine
your eyes would glare hatred at women.
'What a rack, what a sack of trash.'
'She is asking for it.'
'What's your/his/her net worth?'
'Let's network?'
Your nails dug into my palm,
'I'm just trying to stay alive.'
And I think of you now as,
a 6-ft ogre cussing at your own mother
for not cleaning up your defecation
and you wonder, why
everything is so shit-covered.
so here are my last words to you,
you can go burn in Hell,
I won't be joining you.

A Hate Letter to You

He said: I love you.
And it hurt like hell.
He said: I love you.
And my heart filled with mold.
He said: I love you.
And my spine snapped.
He said: I love you.
And my gut crashed.
He said: I love you.
She was there but you weren't.

Hand to head, fist to gut, knife to back,
Slice to wrist.
In words, in words, in words,
we believe.

Shut the fuck up
I don't want your love.

A Disappointing Package

I'm ousting you,
just in case you don't know
what that means;
I'm chucking you out
like dirty laundry
that there is no point to clean.
It means you're that Christmas
sweater I never wanted,
that disappointing pair of socks,
I got when I wanted something special.
Though socks can be useful
you're the wool kind,
the kind I'm allergic to.
You're itchy
and make me wonder, why
I wasn't worth a better gift.
So, I'm ousting you
because you are useless and irritating –
to my toes,
Maybe someone else will enjoy the itch.

The Trouble Is

The trouble is,
I like dancing alone,
I like eating at restaurants without
my portion size being judged,
I like the sound of my voice in my mind,
without you whispering in the background,
I like the way my hands are held by my forearms,
Without being weighed down by yours,
I like seeing a full refrigerator
that hasn't been emptied clean,
I like the rain,
I like standing on my feet
not fearing the fall,
of you dropping me when distracted.
I like knowing my knives are in the cupboard
not used for things they shouldn't be
I like the silence when it isn't in your presence
because it doesn't scream.
I like my sheets clean.
I like sleeping and having soft dreams.
I like kisses that aren't forced,
I like eyes that don't glare.
the trouble is, my once-upon-darling
you are all I have ever had to compare
love to.

The trouble is I prayed for you to leave,
but never opened the door for you
then slammed it shut.
The trouble is, my –once-upon-darling
you leaving was my happy ending
the trouble is, it's gone.

Devil

The devil bores me.
He sits across the table
sipping his tea.
He likes to stare at people
without them noticing
telling me, of things he has said
to so and so.
Like:
'Did you know…?'
'It's just a little white lie.'
'I was joking.'
Ha.
'Why not me?'
The devil is as safe
as an accountant.
He always knows where
every last penny is spent.
Yet, he says things like:
'Yolo.'
'Hey, let's go out!'
Even when I have already said no.
The devil tries
to bend my thoughts
to his desires.
The devil will say

whatever the devil needs
to say to get his way.
The devil is entitled
the devil won't bow down
he fancies himself a god
and sinning in his religious mind
is standing up for yourself.
The devil forbid,
you ever make your own choices
like saying
'I won't go.'
The devil seemed sweet
at first.
He always greeted me with a smile.
But something festers within him
the devil was cordial and friendly too.
Yet I could swear I saw maggots crawling out of his
mouth
he told me he would walk me home.
But the flesh on his chiseled arms chaffed off like wall
paper
the devil kept giving me things.
But the devil came back to reap what he sowed
the devil spoke eloquently.
I have seen him convince the whole room, to give him
their shoes.
Then I heard him speak to himself;
his jealousy seeps through, leaking out
he turns to a puddle of mud.

Faceless Man

To the faceless man
unworthy to be mentioned by name
loving you gave me the title of
'Shit shoveler'
through the endless
amount of anxiety you put me under.
Your memory sits
on me like spit
so I am putting
the thought of you away
I know what you have done
and what cards you have played.
You can lie, lie, lie all you like
eat up everything you see with greed
a goblin dressed in human skin.
Faceless, no matter what car, watch
or brand you wear
my heart is killing the thought of you
white blood cell, macrophages
at the site of infection
I am cleaning up the stain.

Chant

Hum, Hum, Hum.
I've ripped me apart
it's over.
From sinuous that bind meat bone
within the cage of my spirit
I am abstaining from this norm.
Hum, hum, hum
my acute sense of hearing
listens to pages tearing
of ink and blood spilling into rivers
a dawn unsettling
an era ending.
There is no savior but myself.
The layers of life that have been
laid upon me like a block of stone;
it hurts.
Yet I am expected to wash another's
sheets.
The lice are gnawing on my scalp
for their poor hygiene, I have had
to cut my hair
shave it off.
Hum, hum, hum,
I'm leaving you,
The sands move lightly
while the winds blow.

Mirage

No matter how many times
I curse out your name
I can't seem to stop loving it too.
These feelings are nonsense
like walking towards mirages
of I what wish was there but isn't.
I feel thirsty, but you are empty.

Home

Home is a sand dune that has blown away.
I move with the air
with the only roots attached
to me
of my blowing hair.
I have become accustomed
to a Bedouin life
of picking up
what I have
and moving on
where the sand beneath me
shifts
of its own accord.
Home was the promise of snow.
A place I thought I had known.
Home was a place I attributed to your name,
your scent on my sheets
and the sound of you breathing
in morning.
But only a whiff is left
like wafted qoud,
that has gone
to a different place.
Now the fumes belong to another
to me, home was ambergris

in the belly of the whale
that had life but has now
solidified
it smells bitter sweet
of something once living,
but is now dead.
A wish for something eternal
only to discover nothing ever is.
Home was a place I had to leave
pushing myself up
off my knees.
Looking towards a caravan passing by.
Home was a place I thought I belonged,
now all my things are gone.
I move away
from the look in your eyes
they once meant everything
would be fine
now the sound of your voice
has changed.
I walk away from the mirages
of my dreams
knowing something was once mine.

Silence

I waited,
but you withheld
and your silence fell like a slap.
Now you're back
with words I once thought I needed.
like an outfit I have out-grown
your words mean as much to me as a rag
from a ripped, ruffled childhood dress
to small and uncomfortable.
You can keep your words to yourself,
and I will keep mine; they
are too big to be given
to someone as small as you.

Shame

Shame trickles down my skin
of sin
while the rot crawls up the walls
like a smile that slips off
when the doors are closed.
The rot crawls down from the ceiling,
festering.
Loneliness creeps in on my skin.
Your scent suffocates me
the words used to describe me
are heavy
like a body hanging from a noose.
I can't fathom what has just happened.
Maybe I, she, we, all are
what ifs, what ifs, what ifs,
because I shouldn't have
but it happened.
Even if he was the only one
Why? Why? Why am I the only one left?
You have scorched my soul,
and stand I in a trench of self-hatred
living on your words, lulling,
but fake.
They were once my sense of safety
but now I must foster a home.
I am more than my shame.

Distorted

I have given my all; my skin, my hair.
My image reflects back to me
as if it lays on cracked glass,
battered and shook
strike, slap and clap.

Like a cracked egg
yoke spilling
I have spewed my innards
I have no skin, just nerves to touch
taring my mind one pulse at a time.

Ssshhh shhh, you suck up my blood
yet I lay there like a salt screaming leech.
Refuge is darkness
from your tantalizing eyes.
Goodnight.

Y=M+ C

The point of inflection
is the realization
that you are not worth it but I am.
You can shove your love
back into that piece of meat
you call a heart.
You put it up for bidding
and I assume the heiress will win

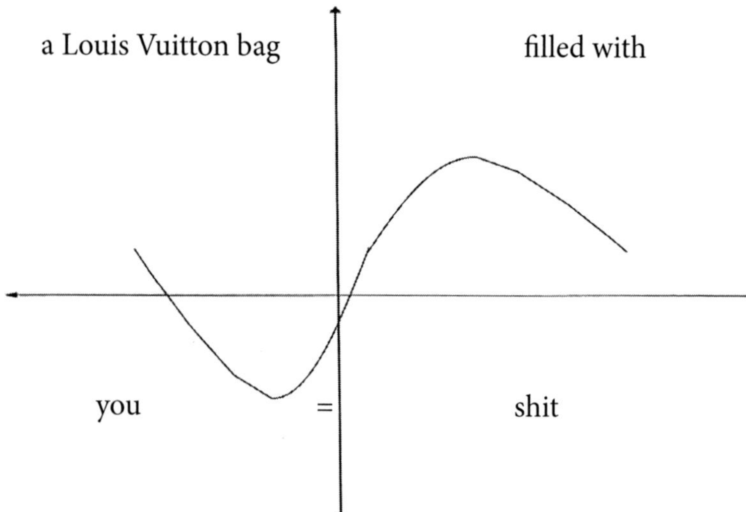

It's Unfathomable to You

I came to you with love
which was a language you never learnt.
I painted you pictures in colors
you refused to see.
I gave you kisses on skin
too scorched to feel.
I sang to you in pitches
you wouldn't hear,
stood empty at the end of it,
deprecated, from a love given
but not received.

Alleyway

In the back of the alleyway
where the feral cats reside
I left your love,
like our unborn love child.
By the grace of all that is good
I hopped on one foot, over,
the corpse of a splintered life,
stumbled out, blurry-eyed and bathed
in the cascade of dawn's light.

Destructum Videbant Venero

I came into this world
with my eyes shut,
to open into
what I should be.
I looked into mirrors
and there the battle began.
I set out to war
with myself, thinking
I was fighting the world.
I tried to concur
the growth of feelings
to bring me, underneath the dogma
of how a human should be.
I lacerated parts of my flesh.
Carving out the muscles in my heart
to fit into what was expected of me.
At the end, I lay there empty,
half human, attempting to
touch the image of perfection.

Trichotillomania

I have been scratching,
picking at my scabs
as my thoughts scalp me from within
to rid the stiches of rules
women as I do bear,
stitched by the fates,
I try to remove the burdens
they have sowed on my skin
I rip out the inscription
transcribed in my behavior
till my nails bleed.

Artichoke

To the many leaves that grew and fell
to kisses and words preserved
in tissues of space.

I'll be wearing black
without the face net for
four months and ten days.

For this departure, I won't be
standing by the train, waving
in high heels, sneakers.

Soul of any kind, I won't be waiting
with my palm up waving
to see a train take you away.

I'll be at home pealing artichokes
nibbling the edges of leaves
waiting to reach the heart.

Weeds

The dawn fell down like ash
I withered, while you grew
leaving me with your emptiness
you took my all
now everything that was beautiful
inside me has died
and I am left weeding out
my chest.

Ashes to Ashes, You Can
Go Fall Apart

A Friend

I have befriended sadness
sometimes he sits next to me
when he needs to.
I have learnt the hard way
to listen to him speak
without interrupting
judging,
expecting,
I accept him for who he is
and he no longer
pursues me, relentlessly.

Sometimes, we sit in silence
at times I speak,
when I need to
but mostly I listen.
We sit watching the sky.

While the gentleness of night sweeps up
like water color into day,
we rest in each other's company,
till it's time for him to leave
I thank him for coming,

what is needed will always be.

Aftershave

I learnt to recognize
what is and what is not
by sniffing,
the scent of your aftershave
in crowds
and walking
the other way.
There will be others,
but the thought of you
will always smell
of citrus and sea to me.

A Chipped Cup

The love I have for you is dying
while you still breathe on me
in memories.
I am burying,
all the things you have chipped
within me,
I am learning to hold another
yet, trying to master carrying myself
like Vancian glass; precious,
delicately, I touch me
without the self-hatred
imprinted from your clumsy hands
I'll try to hold my chalice
high, to love and pour,
into another, without cutting
their lips on
on a chipped tip.

Unboxing

This stuff of moving
it happens quite often,
boxing things up
and unloading the
baggage to move on.
It feels like healing,
settling in your skin.
Unpacking all you have carried
from move to move.
Throwing out that shirt
that doesn't fit or keeping
the broken tea cup to store pencils in
but knowing not to drink out of it.
The process of decluttering
is knowing what serves
and what does not.
It only happens on your terms.
Only you can know
what you need
and what you don't.
It is tiring,
there will be lifting.
There may be dropping.
You will have to cut through
thick duct tape.

Break open the cardboard
with sore hands, arms, and feet.
You may feel weak
but it won't be done.
This is only just the beginning
of the journey
there will be many things
you throw out.
Somethings you'll keep,
unpack into a clear space.
It will be easier to breathe
then you'll find yourself in a new home.
One where you like to be.

FRAGILE

Sobriety

Let sobriety fall upon me
with the understanding of pain
I no longer suffer through the thought of you.
You won't be my crown of thrones.
Nor the hook in my ribs,
creating shafts within me.
I have given—
my all,
my skin, my hair
tethered by a desire
to love and be loved.
I slipped out of
pomegranate-stained sheets
and tied up my hair
I felt the hernia crawl up
my chest
and walked out the door.

Carrying Stones

There are things that can be said to lift up
the human spirit while others act like stones.
These things are phrases to be tucked into
our chests,
and carried with us wherever we go.
The weight of the phrase changes
how we are able to move and how far we can go.
Light words can make whoever
they are given to feel like the can fly.
While the heavy ones
drag our bones down,
sometimes even beneath the ground.

Heal

Let's talk,
have a conversation,
about anything you want to.
We can undress the constraints
of propriety,
you can say what you please to
and I will listen.
Nothing within you is missing,
I have something for you,
words, that act like seeds
to tuck into your chest
and place near your beating center.
You can sow it in your soil.
Should you choose to,
I will help you,
dig deep enough.
You can grow a forest in language.
Pain, doesn't make you barren, these words,

will grow within you
as you become, a little shrub
my little bud.
Should you ever find
someone wilting into themselves
you will have a stalk
from the forest within you
to give to them.

We will bloom out of our misery.

Alone

Everyone has gone home
But I stand under the moonlight
with my soles touching light-kissed streets,
in a dress that drapes down
flowing with the passing breeze.
In the stillness of night
I can hear myself breathe.
My beat guides me
on silky paved roads,
I feel, the ground beneath me
from the tip of my toes to
the cushion of my heels.
I leave.

Forest Child

Behind the foliage,
through the trees
listen closely to the song of the stream,
let your fingers touch the wrinkles of a tree's cheek
you'll feel a draft that lingers on your skin
while the moving wind creates a chime out of leaves.
Through your senses you'll become,
there, you are no longer human
but a spirit that breathes.

The Spirit

The spirits hung from trees
and moved leaves.
Blowing like wind into wandering ears.
While one stepped on wet bark
chipping wood with her foot.
She smelt of musk and blood
wearing a crown of tangled hair.
She ate dragon meat
raw and red, yet her eyes burnt black like coal
she could be seen walking
on the tips of her toes
laughing and laughing
through a hushed howl.
Ripples trickles down her chin,
of words, you thought you heard
but she never said.
She entered.

Kindness

I have heard the kind 'type,'
'nice' type of girls or guys
always finish last.
But this isn't a competition
and a relationship is not the prize,
but love is.
So to all the nice girls and guys,
when you feel like you are taken—
for granted, remember kindness
is love's gentle breath in a soul.
It fills, love's lungs
allowing it to beat and live.
Kindness is,
what somebody and everybody
needs.
And to the girls and guys
who cut up their soul
to fit in.

Just remember, one day
you'll need some kindness
to fill your lungs up
when they empty out.
To resuscitate you
when you feel something within
has stopped beating.
A little kindness, is all
you'll wish for
from someone else.
Even if you have never been kind yourself.
Remember, remember when people
walk on your kindness
and take the air you breathe
rather than give, remember,
my lovely kind-eyed sweetheart,
you are the prize.

قهر

Means paying your dues and others too,
it is a bitter taste
that overpowers all senses.
Like a fish bone stuck in your throat,
of a fine meal eaten by another
but the bill was given to you.
A luxury flaunted in your face
when you have lost all bread
and must sell your bones,
of dreams that cannot be dreamt while
reality clings like a disease,
or a pill that can cure a malady
but the price is your death.
It is the sight of what is needed
but can't be reached
like a man stuffed to the brim,
taking the last bite of a meal
in front of a starving woman.
It is a feeling, a state of being,
it is the reality of many.

Olive Jar

The day I learnt to open the olive jar
It took me a month of attempting.
Stubbornly, my fingers clenching the jar
but then she came
telling me how to hold the knife
and slid it under the lid.
It unleashed the pressure built up.
She stood there with me
fingers holding
the knife together,
I learnt I could do anything.
She told me it wasn't about brute strength
'No, you can do anything
with your own force,
if you know how to.'
She taught me
encouraging me
to unscrew more than just the lid.
Pop, off it came.

I see my rage splatted on pages

Wicked Fate

Through the wreckage that is
the remnants of who I used to be
I will dare to defy my fate
no matter
how hard or cruel.
As I carry the ashes of my old self
in my chest, as an urn.
I will stare into the blinding sun
with my angel-toothed smile
agape.
Even as I scream or cry
I will defy
this woven tapestry laid upon me.
Let the fates stitch misery
into my flesh.
I will laugh at humanity's
twisted dark ways.
Do your worst,
I will retain my soul.

Woman

I go back to my roots
of women who bite –
into liver.
I stand –
with my sword raised
and an arm severed. I,
look you in the eye
coal black,
I will burn you
in a tent
with hay used
for sheep
– befitting –
my soul is teething.
You claim to pray
but spend more time preaching –
decency you lack,
based on your lust,
pouring drool like kerosene
over my body,

and wonder why I hurt you.
My gut is churning
the gale builds up spiraling
I wait, absorbing –
all matter, a witch conjuring – a
hurricane.
horse hooves branding the earth
my grip strengthens
while my other fingers let go
and –
just as wind moves over stone
one day, gently, I'll break your bones.

The Spirit of the Wind

The spirit of the wind
is a dancing child
that feels deeply.
She is the space
between whispers
and fingers.
She moves with words
and finds laugher ticklish.
When she enters
lungs, she pushes them
in – out.
She, is the first contact
before lips
part to meet
and skin is caressed.
She can feel disappointment in sighs
and the abrasiveness
of all that is loud.
She understands.
Yet, she, can rip you apart
with gentleness,
she pushes
the spaces between
sheets of skins and atoms.
Her quietude can silence

all mouths,
grabbing, breath away.
She is intangible
and her bonds are frail.
Yet, she is the movement
that rips out mountains,
carries fire
she stirs the storm
when she chooses to.
The spirit of the wind
is a female who has embraced herself.

Killdeer Dance

You,
pour into my ravine
with disregard for my need of space.
You,

crouch down on me
my soil to acid filled muck.
Your contents itch me
I,

snatch up crawlers with my beak snapping,
voice piercing.
Shrill kill dee-dee-deer
I preform the killdeer dance
broken winged hopping
taking your gaze away.
I am,
gulping down your wormy minions
unravelling the seams of the earth
meant as a proposal.
I unthread you from my soil.

Beasts of Burden

I am the beast of burden
harnessed to be tamed
to carry the weight
of your ego.
A female is no more than
a mule to you, to sit on and use.
Your words dangle in front of me,
promises hung like a carrot on a stick.
Every gesture is a means to an end with you
why else would you be decent?
I won't carry your insecurities
and needs on my back,
I'm bucking you off.

I saw, I heard, I walked away.

Hammurabi's Code

An eye for an eye
and a heart for a heart.
You've sucker punched me
in the chest.
I see you smirking when I blush
and to that I say, should I fall,
I shall drag you down with me.

The Debate

He tells me he is a dragon
and I tell him I am butterfly
to which he retorts snorting
at my gentleness
and I, resilient eye to his eye, say:
'At least I am real,
should dragons have ever been
butterflies out-lived the legend
of your greatest ambition.
Your strength is every bit as
a tale as its expression
– unreal and imagined –
so go puff out the hot air you are made of, love.
I will carry on wafting through the breeze
feeling the light of day.'

He Makes Me Smile

He makes me smile, despite myself.
He makes me smile, through a face
full of scars, I feel beautiful,
my jaw taking a form it hasn't in years,
for reasons it has never known.
He makes me smile,
despite myself.
I find myself, enjoying his words
but not needing any specific ones to be said.
He makes me smile,
because he just is, who he is,
as he is.
He makes me smile.
As I am, I can bring forth happiness,
and we share it,
in a moment, in a word
in a smile.

I Wrote You a Poem Today

I tried to write you a poem
I nearly tucked it
into a sonnet, till
I realized enjambment
expressed my distorted
thoughts on you –
creating the tension
releasing it
only rhythm and rhyme
can express the movement
between us
a space undefined
without closure.

Figments of My Imagination

I keep falling in love,
with a figment of imagination
but you should know it isn't easy.
It takes a good dose of delusion
coupled with free time and
a tendency towards escapism.
Some would call it courageous
to venture into a magical world where
anything, just anything could happen.
Others would think it's insane
but you see,
It takes skill to lose touch
with reality.
When I look at you, I see
your words are pouring like milk
through a sieve
I haven't been listening,
my mind's been wandering
I've stolen your face and given it
to a character I have made up
in my head.

I think I might like him better.
I put words into your mouth
without caring about
what actually comes out.
Who needs the reality
of anyone's character
when fantasy is far more intriguing
and kinder?
Sure, we can be lovers
just stick to the script.
What was your name again?

Cracked

He has fallen in love
with my brokenness
my cracks make him feel
whole, intact, he bids
himself some savior
hasn't figured out
we are all damaged.
He looks into mirrors
without perceiving –
he is trying to save me
without realizing
I belong to the birds.
The crows stand as
my only compatriots.

I Let Go

I broke his heart.
He had too much blue
he was made for the sky
and I am the essence of brown,
land bound and
tied.
I keep reaching into the softness
of the sky
but I can't have it
so, I let go.

Annuals

The flowers are stripping,
slipping out of their buds.
Fluffy fans of petals fall out.
The stems stand nude.
wilting under the pressure
of windy weather.
Declaring, 'You have seen it all.'
It crumbles down to the ground.
The blank soil canvas eats it up.
The last bit of color
offered to its mouth.
The earth hardens with the wait
for the new season
in anticipation of little buds sprouting out.
Sweetly, it supports them up
for the season.
A youthful face paces by the field
tears out their roots,
to ask,
'He loves?'
'She loves me not?'

How I Will Love You

Oh, how I will love you
when I find you
should we meet on the street
in a lamp shop,
post office,
book store,
buying groceries
we walk down different aisles.
Oh my love, I can imagine
you climbing a mountain range,
helping a child in need
or tracing your fingers on a braille sheet.
Oh my love, how I will love you
when I find you
even if you are confused,
speak another language
or you're a stranger passing by
in the street.
Oh my love, how I will love
even if you are not a boy
have scars on your thighs,
from knives, paper cuts
or scissors
despite how much you have tried.
My love, I will love you
when I find you.
P.S. Look for me too.

Meadow

You've whisked me away
on a midnight river ride,
I'll wear the moonlight
as we dance through a meadow
under a universe of stars
I was running away
in my one-woman Bedouin caravan
singing songs to guide me
through the night.
Stepping
on the silk of sands, we met
you were a wind rider
looking for another fight
with fire.
You carried candle light,
lanterns, torches of any kind.
Kissing the parts that ache
we burn together
now, lift up the light
and let me
look inside.

Flutter

He is trying to catch my fluttering spirit
using spells and charms
in foreign languages
he has learnt.
He straddled me down
tearing out pages of pledges
I have written to myself.
I have taken a vow;
he is breaking it.
He looks like
he is on a Moroccan high
enchanted by my dancing
he tells me stories
of a thousand and one nights.

Conversations

You think I am immigrant,
perhaps you smelt
the scent of cinnamon and turmeric
lingering on my skin
and you have been picking on my mouth
for holding words
yours can't seem to produce,
like a baby *cou, cou, cou*
you think I have to come to stay in your land
why else would I sit here across the table
from you?
Attempting to share a life with you.
You stare at me with a look
of intrigue.
And I sigh at you with disbelief
at how you can just not understand.
Though roots and soil lay between us
your eyes are always so direct and curious
mine drift off –
into thoughts
yet something else crawls in
between us –
in frustration of what cannot be had
you say things like,
'Here in Europe.'

And I feel like my heterogeneous origins are
alien, for being Syrian,
middle eastern.
A refugee, is that what you think of me?
Then you apologize
'Oh, I am sorry I have offended you.'
Yes, you have
but not because of your curiosity.
Always probing into me
deeper and deeper
and I try to hold up my cup gracefully
and explain patiently;
I am human too.
Looking into your brown eyes
as earthy as mine.
Can't you see,
what I am trying to say
in a foreign language, even to me
is, I love you.

Irritation

When I think of you
I think of friction
– you irritate me,
majestically –
yes, I am drawn
to you – in
anger – in confusion.
You have a way
of, let's say
– playing –
with words
with nerves
pinching spots
– you shouldn't –
and then smiling
but it's more of a sneer
clear as it may be
you're doing it on purpose
I feel like I am teething
with desire – to bite –
but I won't take the bait
go ahead and sneer
I'll continue to strut.

Linger I

Darling, let's linger.
Let's let our finger tips touch
without –
holding hands.
Let's breath on each other's skin, without,
parting our lips to speak.
Let's move towards each other,
but always maintain a foot apart,
a heartbeat apart.
Let's look at each other
and drift, away –
when our pupil's meet.
Let's just be.

Linger II

Darling, let's linger
let your fingers,
fall into mine.
Let your heart beat
a little faster each time.
Lips parted, with each breath you take
in pace –
It might take time,
for your skin to feel the warmth inside.
Cadence, is love's true form.
Let's start soft and slow.
Hard-er
let us transform.

Orange

Hey there, easy peeler,
vital and sweet
I want you
every day.
You taste like
a soft roll
on my tongue,
warm cinnamon,
something forbidden.
From across the table
newspapers flipping,
coffee cups clupping onto
tables of people beginning their day.
Across the room our eyes meet.

You're a Raccoon

My raccoon masked lover
I find you bumping into a bin
tin stuck on your snout.
Peevish, restless
you express your love like a hiccup
you can kiss,
the marshmallow-cover
that pad my bones
I won't make any startling moves
to frighten you back into your den.
Washing your hands, a hundred times
they smell just fine,
but my food has gone missing
you have left your shirt behind
and crumbs on the floor.
I guess, you'll be back for your belongings,
which are actually my things.
Don't worry, you don't snore
instead of creeping around at night
you can come in
and switch on the light.

Game

Let's play a game,
where we try to make each other ache.
The goal is to be caressed
and smell the scent of warm breath,
eyelashes brushing upon skin.
Come in,
there are no doors, only fabric
to rip and tear.
Let us shatter our bones
against each other until,
we exhale.
We surrender to each other
with our lips.

Kisses

come with tenderness
and let it shift
into my space
kisses   kisses   kisses   kisses
kisses   kisses kisses   kisses
kisses
kisses   kisses   kisses
kisses kisses kisses kisses *kisses* kisses
kisses kisses
kisses
kisses kisses
kisses kisses
kisses kisses kisses kisses over

all the places that ache.

A Crush

I would like to
unravel you.
Hurt you,
with kisses,
cause you
to ache
and then break
the silence
of your stare,
blue, sharp, and sparkling
like water,
bubbly,
you pain me, making me
nauseous.
And I, am not one to take
an assault, in silence,
as you smirk knowingly
testing me.
In words and fleeting caresses
in a haphazard manner.
I have come to crave you.

Knight

In a moment
the dress slips
down my knees
to the floor.
Heal me, with words
that dress like knights
to fight
the ones I was once told.
I want you
to touch me
but have learnt
to feel scared
of finger tips
other than my own.
I like it,
when you play with my hair.
Or look me in the eye.
Even if I know you can't
conquer my battels
with words or swords.
Only my thoughts can
win.
Then I stand there
in a moment,
in a dress that slips down to my knees, I feel whole.

Safe

I return to myself with safety,
undres^si^ng,
I u n d o all,
I have tied up
like loose rope fallin^g

dropp^n ig
I am releasing the inner fl^ut^er
to find my peace.
I say things –
Softly, come embrace me,
I have arrived
home in my skin
after being gone for so long
l^ost, I find myself,
I meet me with gratitude
of a life ¹ lived
of my own vol^it^ion
rid myself,

of anything that feels too ti^{gh}t
I throw my shoes of^{f}
and stand with b a r e
feet walking, on sand to meet the sea
that rides in my chest
I find my dep^{t}hs.
Within them lay
Th^{u}nder, blo^{o}ming fl^{o}wers
and p^{o}uring
rain.

Pillow Forts

We are slipping out of our clothes,
coffee stains our teeth
clanging cups and our bodies together
to toast.
Falling off the edge of our bed
breaking a pillow fort
fluffy dough,
won't muffle our singing,
we crumble up foil into heart-shaped casts.
Last night's dinner is heated again.
We munch every last bite.
Sharing a kaki snack,
we let the juice drip down our chins,
you grin, with lipstick
that marks you unknowingly.
We walk out with clacking heels
and closing-opening doors
'I love you's,' 'I love you's.'
We rumble through each day
till we tumble back into our bed
under our pillow fort.

The Stars

The stars are falling
I am willing to walk into love.
They sparkle endlessly
you have swept me up.
Shooting through a moving sky
in the gust of your eyes.
The world wafts by.
Your smile is dazzling.
I await midnight.
My heart is shimmering
For the brilliant flutter of light.

Come

Breathe on me
I'll fight you back with kisses.
In a moment of color
we merge, creating,
dancing, along to the sounds
of the hu-u-u-u-m in our throats.
I want to hear you croak.
You coax me back, with fingers
that caress me,
darling, undress me.